MW01658247

What Is Weather?

by Carol Levine

PEARSON
Scott Foresman
DK

Measuring Weather

What is it like outside where you live? What is the **weather** like today?

Weather changes all the time. Is it wet or dry? Are there clouds? Can you see the Sun? Is there wind? How hot or cold is it?

It is cold here.

It is hot here.

Temperature is how hot or cold something is. Temperature changes. We measure temperature using numbers.

The temperature is a higher number when it is hot. The temperature is a lower number when it is cold.

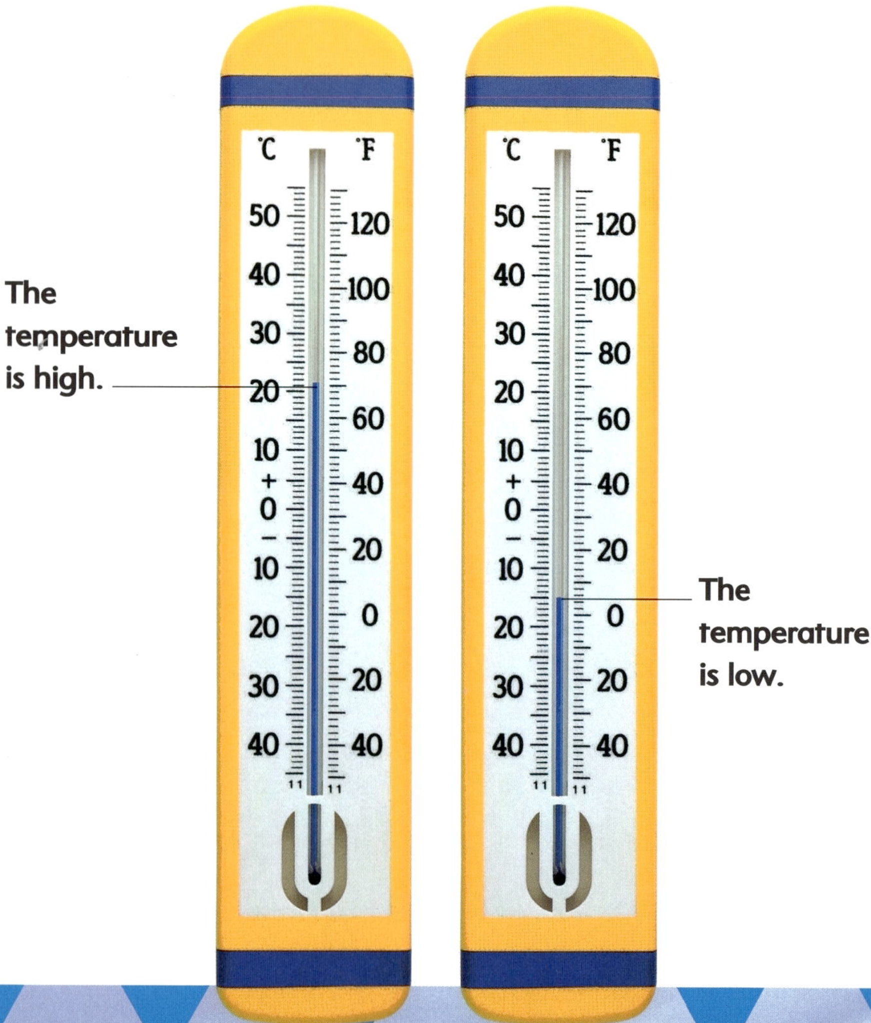

Weather Tools

There are many weather tools. A **thermometer** tells the temperature. It shows the numbers.

A wind vane tells which way the wind is blowing. A snow gauge tells how much snow falls. A rain gauge tells how much rain falls.

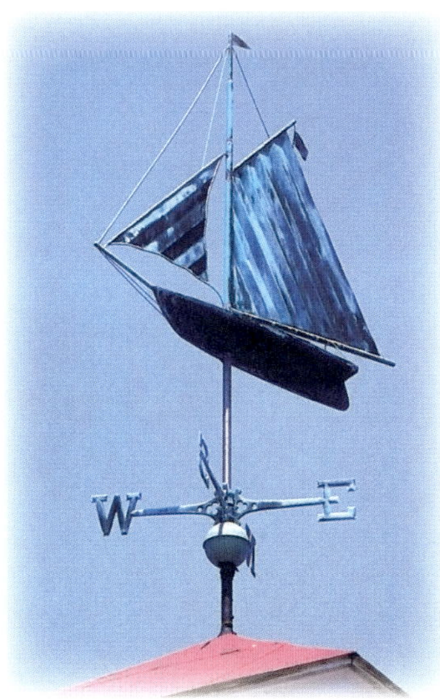

Wind vane

Rain gauge

Clouds

Water vapor is water in the air. You cannot see water vapor.

Clouds are made when water vapor cools. **Clouds** are made of many tiny drops of water or ice.

There are many different kinds of clouds. Different clouds bring different weather. Most high clouds mean good weather. Most low clouds mean bad weather. Very low clouds make fog.

High clouds

Wet Weather

There are different kinds of wet weather. Wet weather can help living things. Plants need water from wet weather. But many living things look for shelter from wet weather.

Rain

Rain is a kind of wet weather. Some living things want to stay dry when it rains.

Sleet

Sleet is a kind of wet weather. Rain can turn to sleet when it is cold. **Sleet** is rain that freezes.

Snow

Snow is a kind of wet weather. Snow is water that freezes high in the air. It falls from the clouds when it is very cold. Many living things look for warm shelter when it snows.

There are different kinds of snowstorms. There is lots of snow in a blizzard. Light snow that falls for a short time is called a flurry. A snow burst has lots of snow that falls quickly.

Seasons

A **season** is a time of year. There are four seasons each year. They are spring, summer, fall, and winter. The seasons always come in the same order.

Spring

Summer

Seasons have different weather in different places. Spring can be warm. Summer can be hot. Fall can be cool. Winter can be cold. Winter can be very cold in some places.

Fall

Winter

Seasons change in a pattern. Spring is before summer. Summer is before fall. Fall is before winter. Winter is before spring. Then the pattern starts again.

Weather is always changing. Living things find ways to live in all kinds of weather.

Look out the window. See what the weather is now. What do you think the weather will be tomorrow?

Glossary

clouds	shapes in the sky made of tiny water drops or pieces of ice
season	one of the four times of the year
sleet	rain that freezes
temperature	how hot or cold something is
thermometer	a tool to measure the temperature
water vapor	water as a gas in the air
weather	what it is like outside